STICKER STUDIO

# APOTHECARY

a sticker gallery

*for*

modern mystics

CASTLE POINT BOOKS

NEW YORK

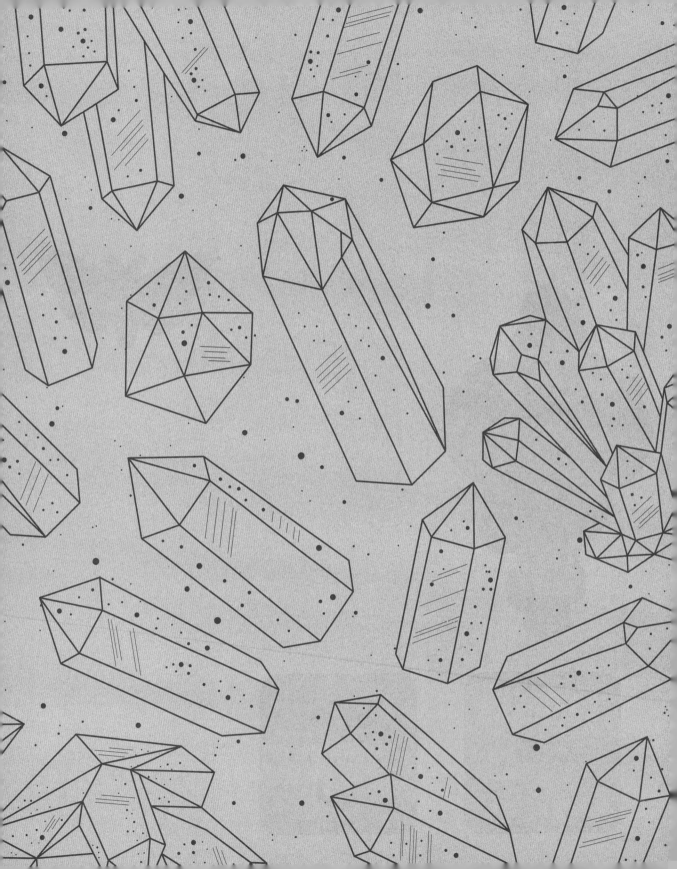

Nature's peace will flow
into you as sunshine
flows into trees.

—*John Muir*

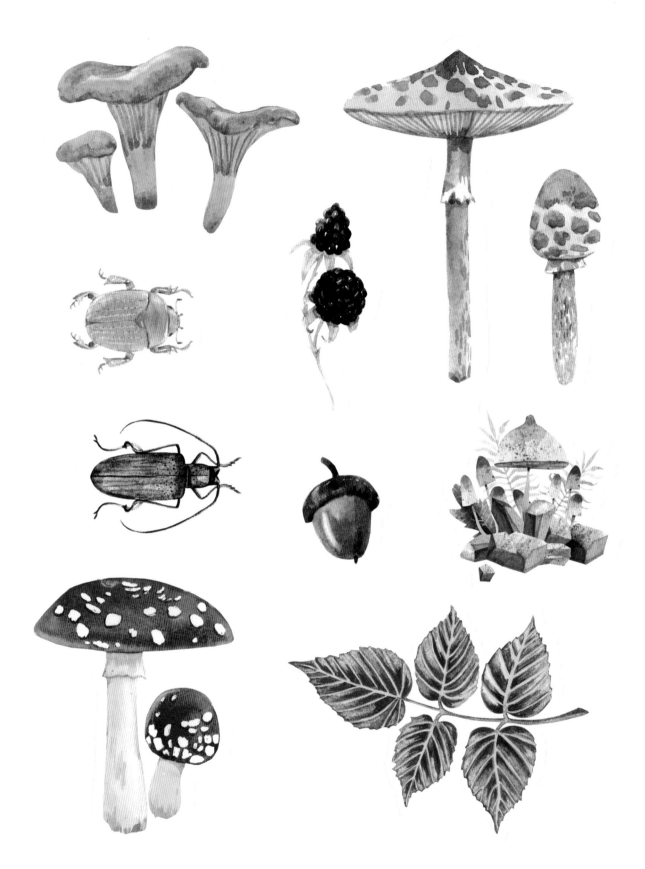

Everything in nature
invites us constantly
to be what we are.

—*Gretel Ehrlich*

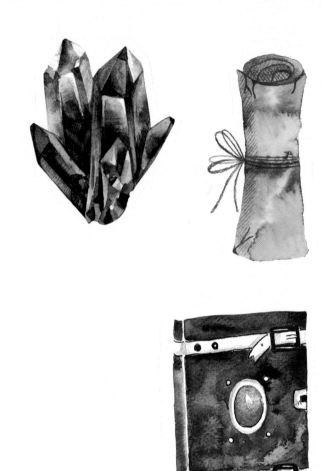

Think of all the beauty still left
around you and be happy.

—*Anne Frank*

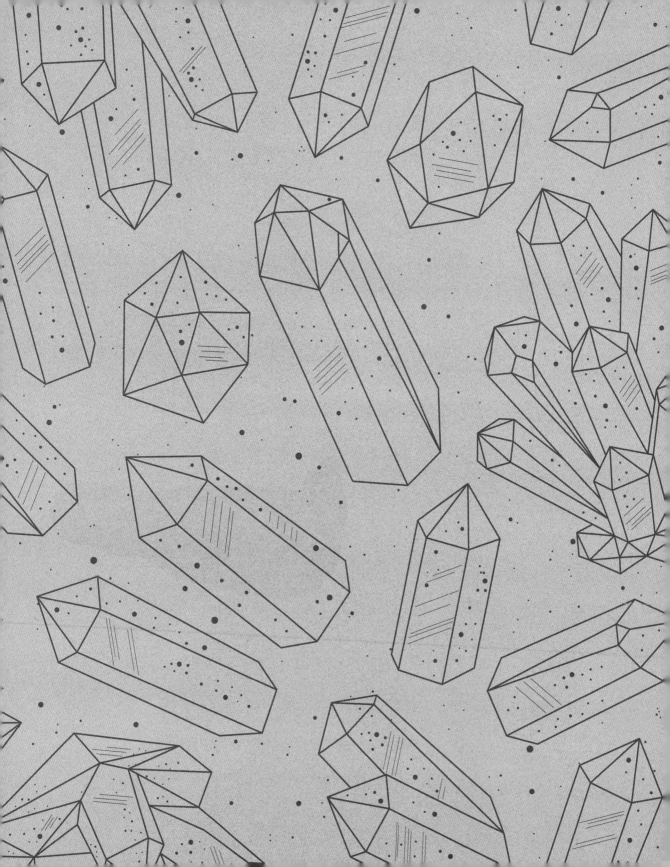

There's a resonance inside
us, a sense of who we are. We're
a multi-bodied traveler. We're an
essence. We're a feeling, an awareness
that has an ancient existence.

—*Frederick Lenz*

Beauty in things exists
in the mind which
contemplates them.

—David Hume

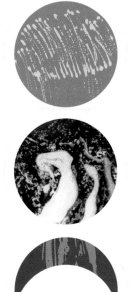

Nothing can cure the soul but the senses, just as nothing can cure the senses but the soul.

—*Oscar Wilde*

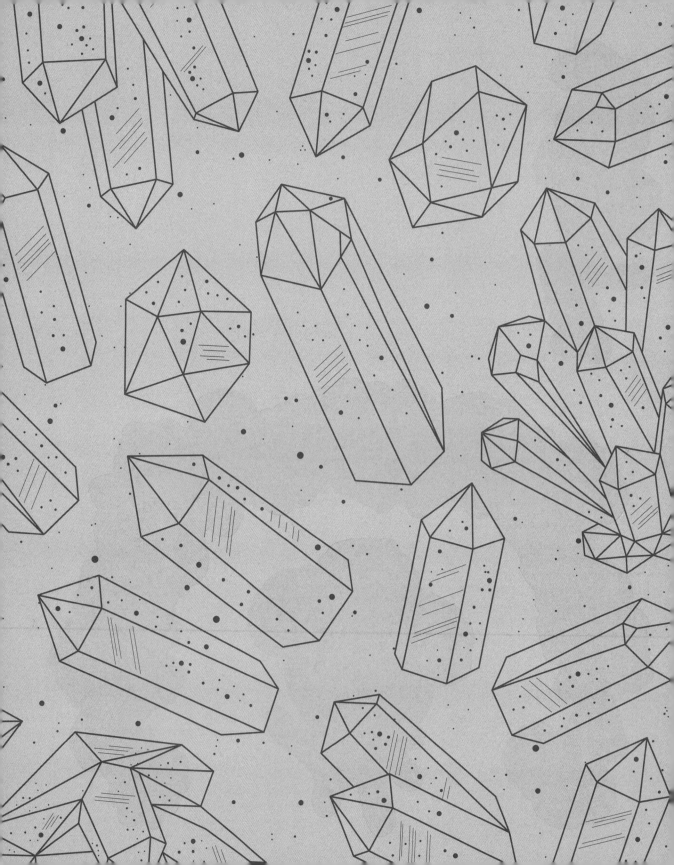

When you take a flower in your
hand and really look at it, it's
your world for the moment.

—*Georgia O'Keeffe*

It is not so much for its beauty
that the forest makes a claim upon men's
hearts, as for that subtle something, that quality
of air that emanation from old trees, that so
wonderfully changes and renews a weary spirit.

—*Robert Louis Stevenson*

All good things are
wild and free.

—Henry David Thoreau

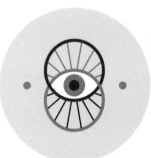

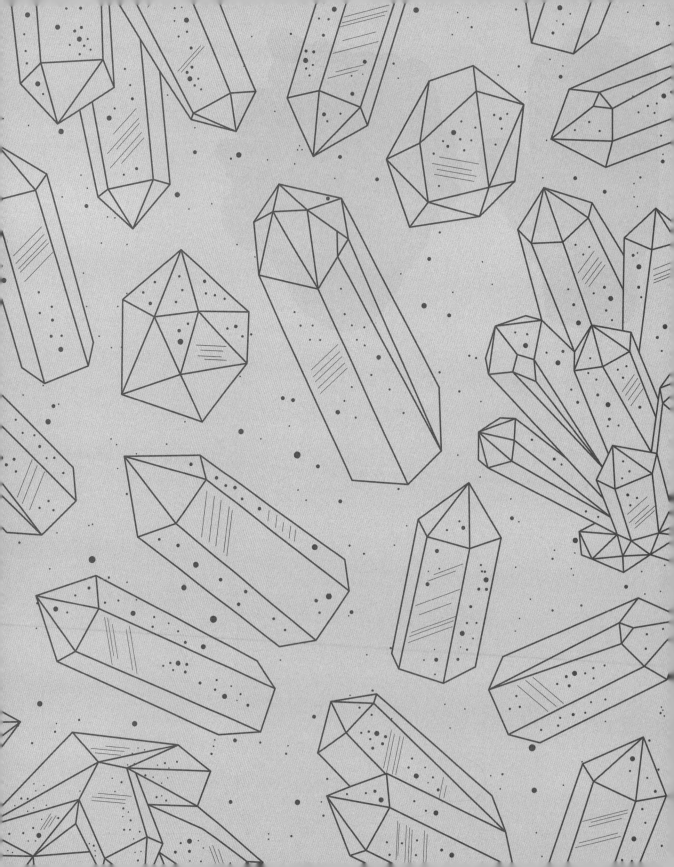

I will soothe you and heal you,
I will bring you roses.
I too have been covered with thorns.

—*Rumi*

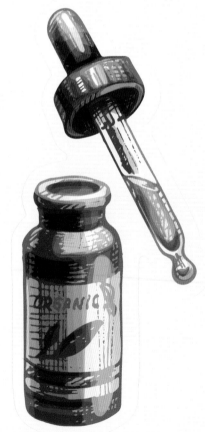

We must close our eyes and invoke a new manner of seeing, a wakefulness that is the birthright of us all, though few put it to use.

—*Plotinus*

The simple things are also the
most extraordinary things, and
only the wise can see them.

—*Paulo Coelho*

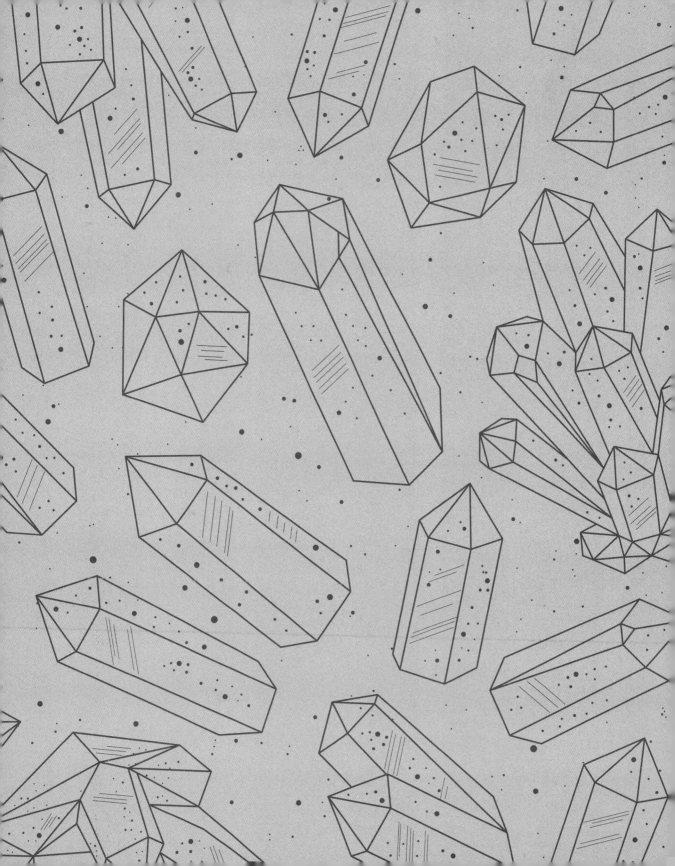

The gravitational pull of
the mystical is stronger
than that of gravity.

—*Rajesh*

Beauty of whatever kind, in its supreme development, invariably excites the sensitive soul to tears.

—*Edgar Allan Poe*

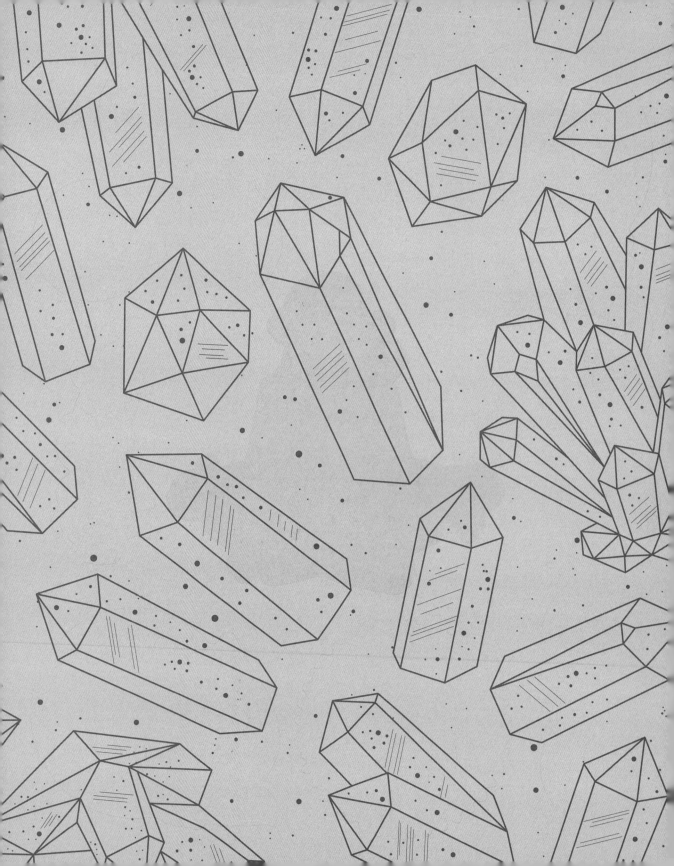

Every man is more than just himself; he also represents the unique, the very special and always significant and remarkable point at which the world's phenomena intersect, only once in this way, and never again.

—*Hermann Hesse*

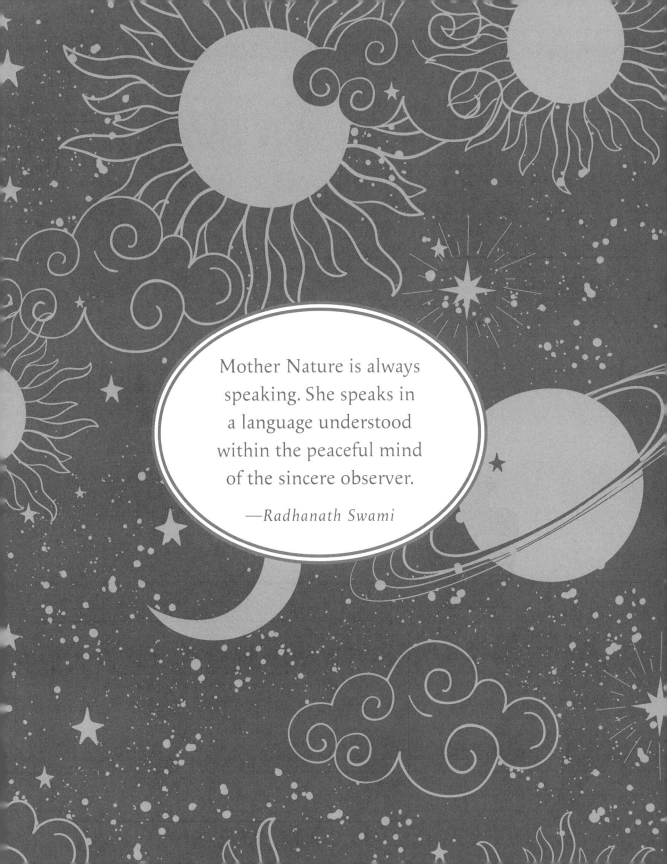

Mother Nature is always speaking. She speaks in a language understood within the peaceful mind of the sincere observer.

—Radhanath Swami

# Mrs. Pomeroy's

*Pathetic Pumpkins*

Small, but handsome!
Slightly scary, slightly scared.
Not edible. Definitely not.
Owl delivery the very same day.

Complete catalogue available now.

33, Old Bucket St. W., London

WITCHING HOUR
DON'T BE LATE

POTION
No 9

# MAGICAL DETECTIVES

Got cursed or bewitched?
Lost one of your socks or a friend?

## FALCONETTI & SONS

PRIVATE INVESTIGATORS

(We'll find you instead.) LONDON

# GRIMOIRES
### RARE AND DUSTY BOOKS

grimoires · used school books · magic maps
**THE WHOLE WORLD OF WIZARDRY IN ONE STORE!**

Grindelwald's Grimoires · 42, Buckled Bug Road, LONDON

BELLA BAKER'S BEWITCHING FRUITS AND POTIONS ARE MADE WITH CARE AND LOADS OF WITCHCRAFT. FRUITS HARVESTED IN A FULL MOON. TAKE CARE!

BELLA BAKER'S BEWITCHING
**DEADLY**
# NIGHTSHADE
ORGANIC SQUASH AND JUICE

# BEETLEJUICE
with a slice of woodlouse
### THE TASTE OF CRAWLING CRITTERS!
Beetlejuice is a healthy and natural refreshment without any nasties.
Containing chitin. Shake well and serve chilled.

CONTAINS **NATURAL FLAVORS ONLY**

prize-winning producer · successful since 1822

**THE LITTLE BUGGER**, Main Graveyard, left

*Dr. Plummer's*
# PECULIAR POTIONS
### SURPRISE EFFECT GUARANTEED!
simply send us one of your owls *or* come over to the doctor's office

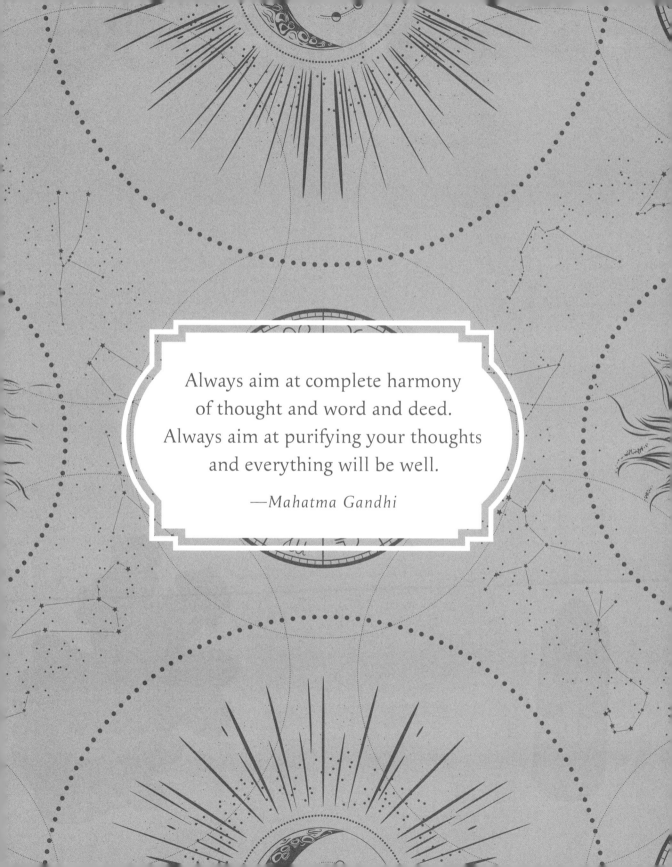

Always aim at complete harmony
of thought and word and deed.
Always aim at purifying your thoughts
and everything will be well.

—*Mahatma Gandhi*

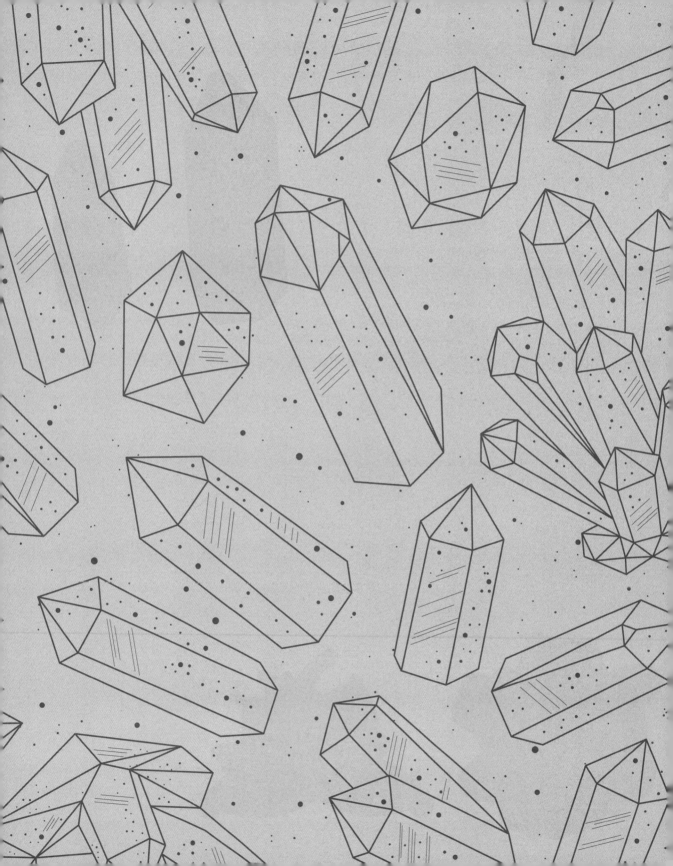

May love and light prevail. May
divine wisdom reign supreme. May
it transform the darkness; and heal
the realms where shadows dwell.

—*Anthon St. Maarten*

The knowledge of all
things is possible.

—*Leonardo da Vinci*

Nature does not hurry, yet
everything is accomplished.

—*Lao Tzu*

The most effective paths
to soul are nature-based.

—*Bill Plotkin*

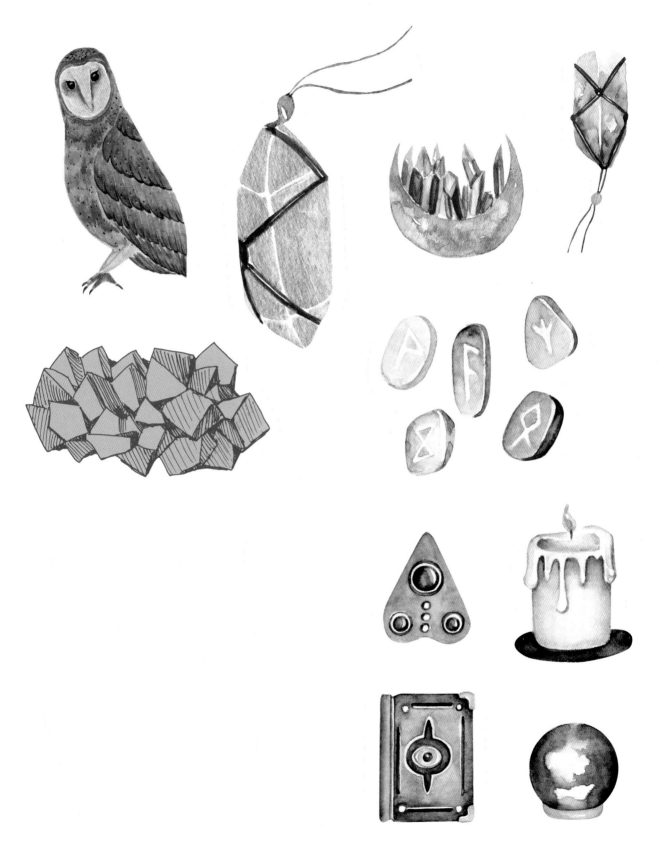

Just living is not enough.
One must have sunshine,
freedom, and a little flower.

—*Hans Christian Andersen*

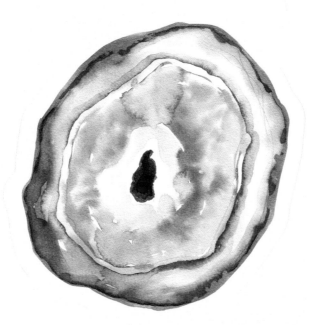

My soul can find no staircase
to heaven unless it be
through Earth's loveliness.

—*Michelangelo*

The power of finding
beauty in the humblest
things makes home
happy and life lovely.

—*Louisa May Alcott*

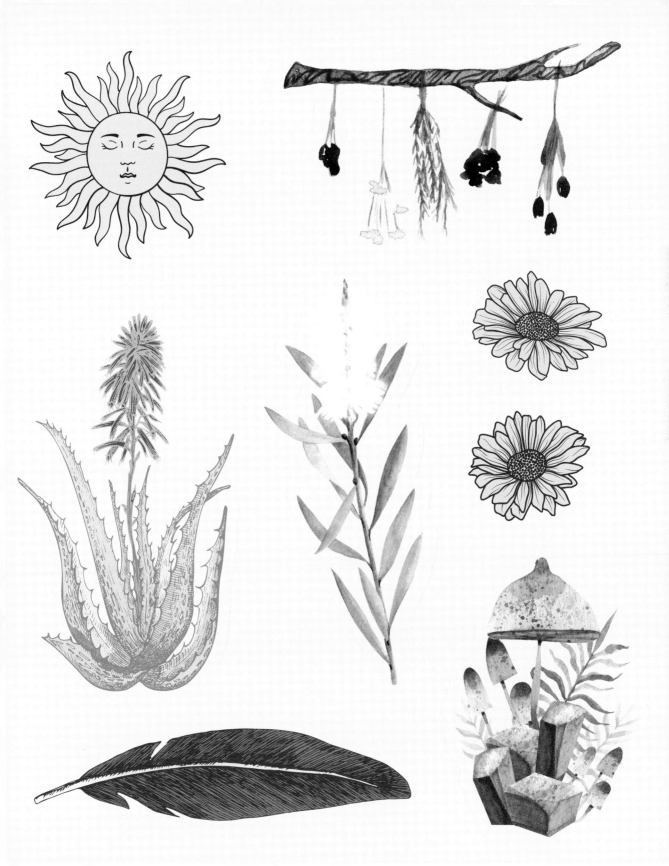

I believe the world is
incomprehensibly beautiful
— an endless prospect
of magic and wonder.

—*Ansel Adams*

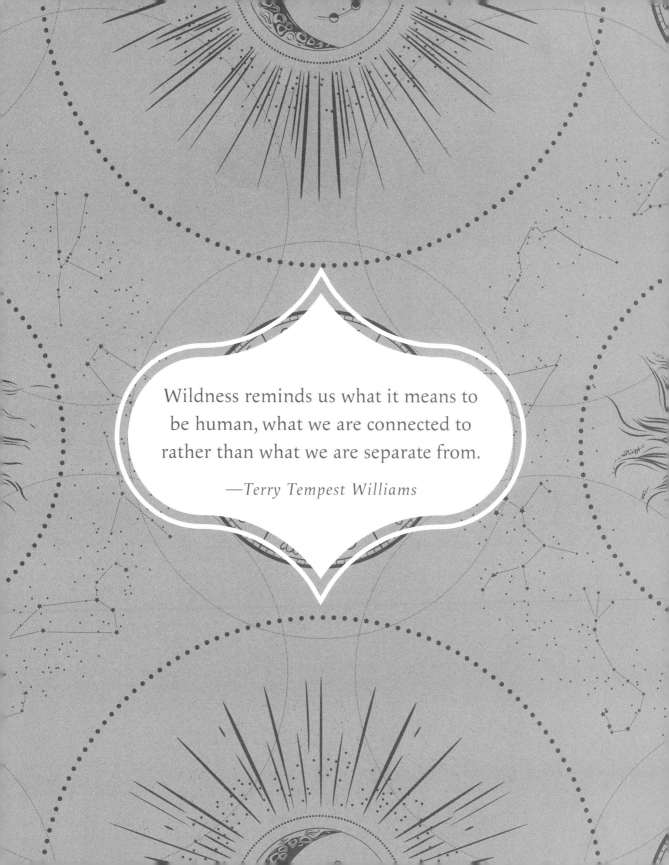

Wildness reminds us what it means to be human, what we are connected to rather than what we are separate from.

—*Terry Tempest Williams*

It is good to know our
universe. What is new
is only new to us.

—*Pearl S. Buck*

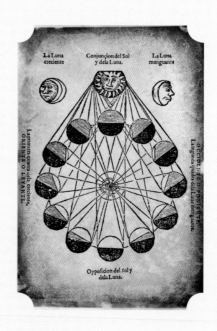
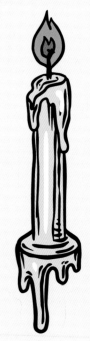

One of the first conditions
of happiness is that the link
between man and nature
shall not be broken.

—*Leo Tolstoy*

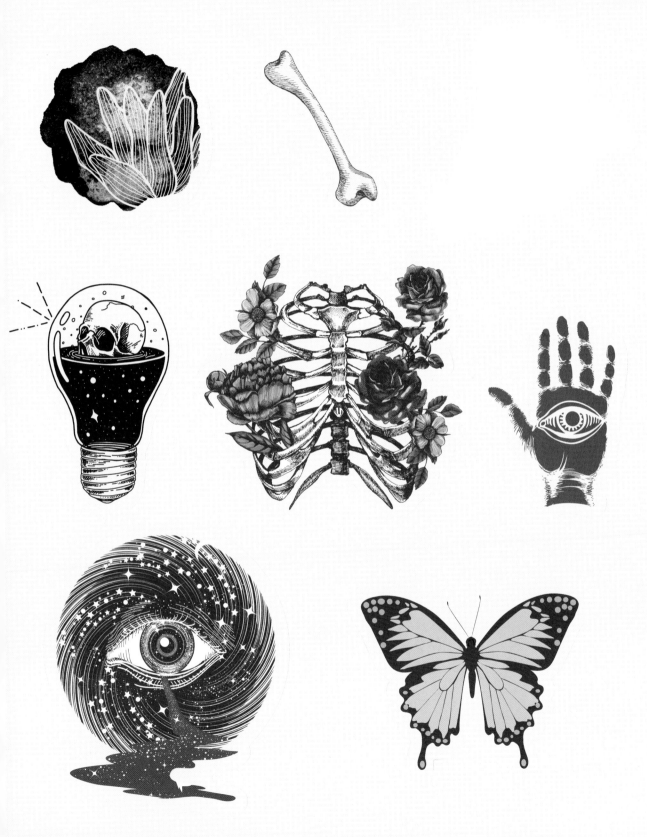

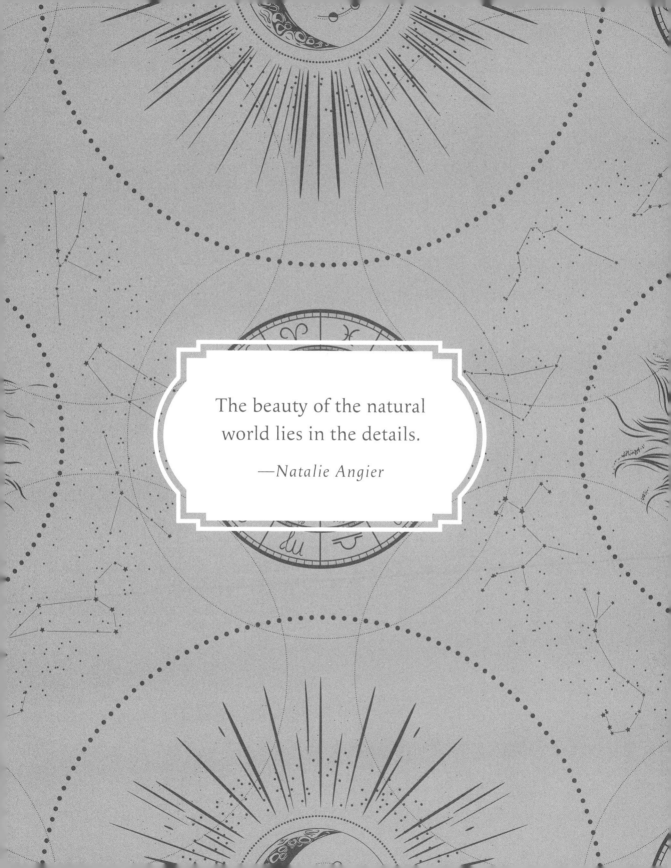

The beauty of the natural
world lies in the details.

—*Natalie Angier*

*Amanita muscaria*　　　Agaricales

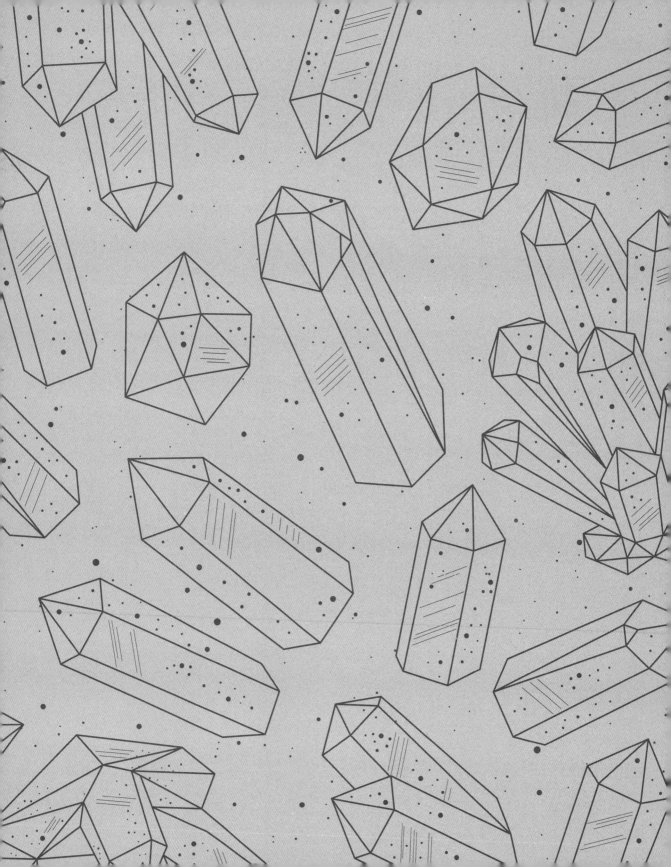

I go to nature to be
soothed, healed, and have
my sense put in order.

—*John Burroughs*

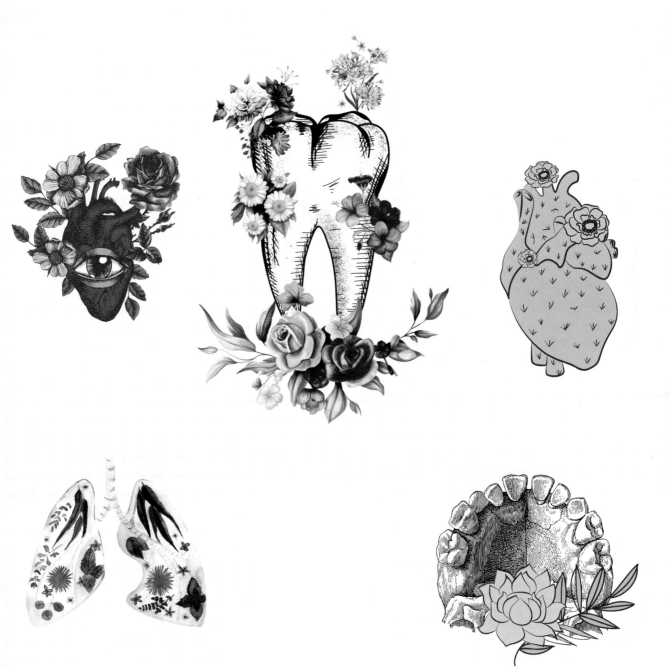

To sit in the shade on a fine day, and look upon the verdure is the most perfect refreshment.

—*Jane Austen*

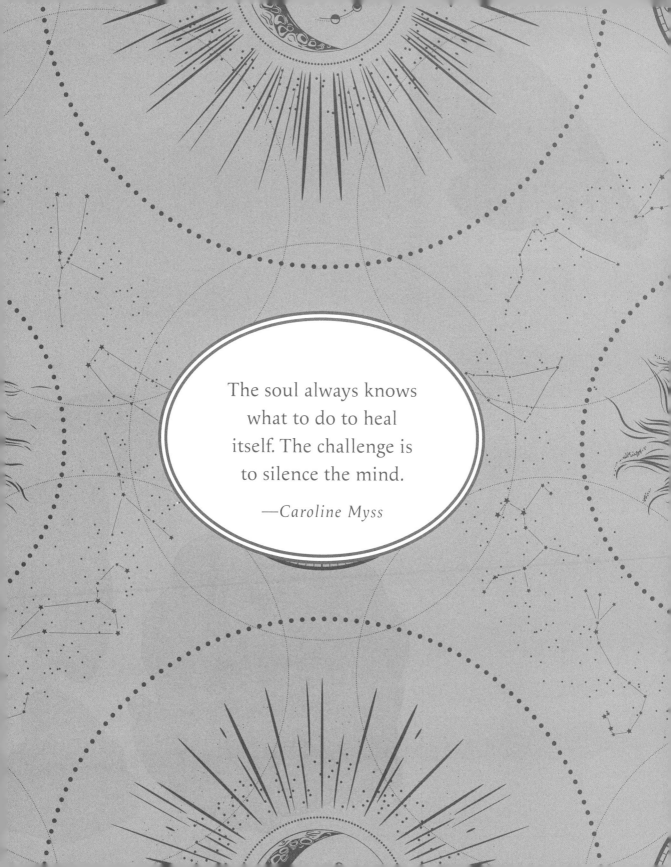

The soul always knows
what to do to heal
itself. The challenge is
to silence the mind.

—*Caroline Myss*

The rhythm of the body, the
melody of the mind, and the
harmony of the soul create
the symphony of life.

—B.K.S. Iyengar

Adopt the pace of nature.
Her secret is patience.

—*Ralph Waldo Emerson*

www.castlepointbooks.com

The Castle Point Books trademark is owned by Castle Point Publishing, LLC.
Castle Point books are published and distributed by St. Martin's Publishing Group.

ISBN 978-1-250-27934-7 (paper-over-board)

Design by Melissa Gerber
Images used under license from Shutterstock

Our books may be purchased in bulk for promotional, educational, or business use.
Please contact your local bookseller or the Macmillan Corporate and Premium Sales Department
at 1-800-221-7945, extension 5442, or by email at MacmillanSpecialMarkets@macmillan.com.

First Edition: 2021

10 9 8 7 6 5 4 3 2